W9-ABC-564

How a Seed Grows

by Helene J. Jordan

illustrated by Joseph Low

THOMAS Y. CROWELL COMPANY   New York

A seed is a little plant.
It is a plant that has not
started to grow.

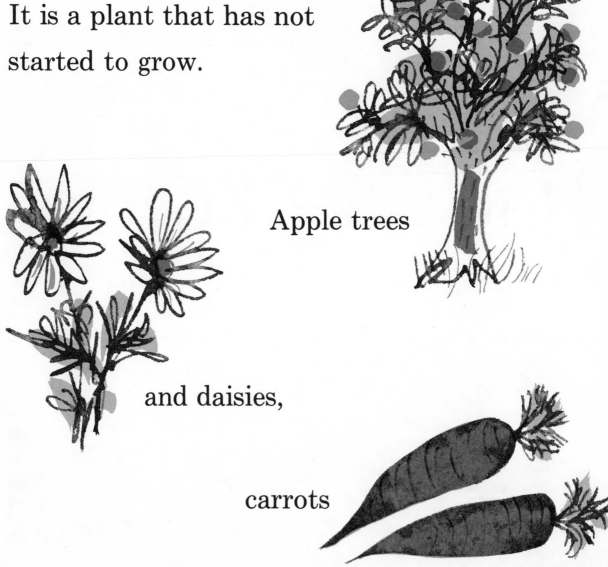

Apple trees

and daisies,

carrots

2

and corn,

clover

and wheat,

all grow from seeds.

Here is a tree seed.

Some day it will be
a tree like this.

Here is a flower seed.

Some day
it will be a flower
like this.

Some seeds grow slowly.

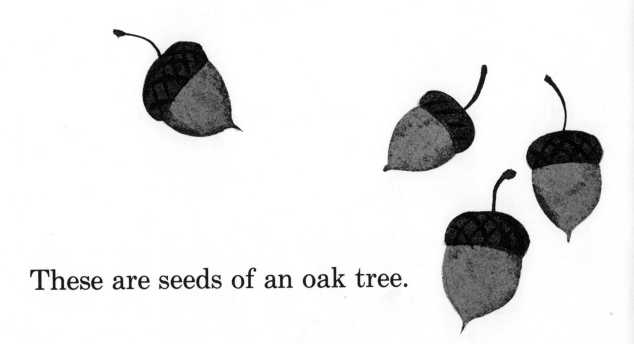

These are seeds of an oak tree.

An oak tree grows very, very slowly.

This is how slowly it grows.

Suppose you planted an oak tree seed.

You would be a father, or a mother,
or even a grandfather, or a grandmother
and the oak tree would still be growing.

9

Some seeds grow fast.

This is a bean seed.

It grows very fast.

It grows so fast that it becomes a bean plant
in just a few days.

You can plant bean seeds yourself.

You can plant them in egg shells.

You can plant them in tin cans

or old cups

or little flower pots.

We used egg shells.

We filled ten egg shells with soil like this.

We made a hole in the soil with a finger, like this.

You can do it, too.

When you have made
a hole in the soil,
plant a bean seed in it.

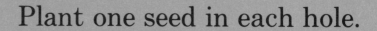

Plant one seed in each hole.

Cover the seed with soil.

Food for the seed is in the soil.

Sprinkle the soil
with a little water.

Number the shells.

Put the number 1  on the first shell.

 Put the number 2 on the next shell.

Put the number 3 on the next shell.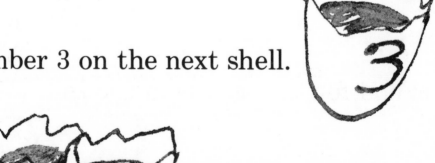

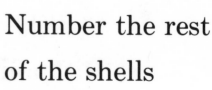 Number the rest
of the shells

until they are numbered from 1 to 10.

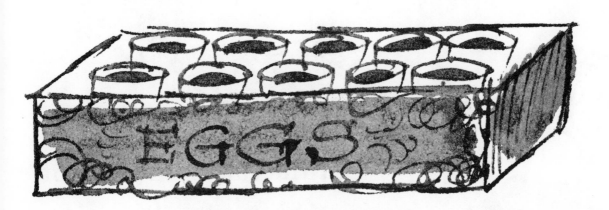

Put all the egg shells in an egg carton.

Put the carton in sunlight
on a window sill.

Some bean seeds grow faster than others.

Our seeds began to grow in three days.

Your bean seeds may start to grow in two days.

They may take longer before they start to grow.

Watch your seeds.

Water them
a little
every day.

The water soaks into the seeds.

The seeds begin to grow.

More water soaks into the seeds.

The seeds get fatter and fatter.

Wait for three days

and then dig up
seed Number 1.

It may be soft. It may be fat.

Maybe it will look the same as it did before.

Soon the seed will grow so fat that its skin
will pop off.

In two more days
dig up seed Number 2.

Maybe it will look different now.
Maybe the skin of this seed will be loose.

Now a root starts to grow.

The root grows from one end of the bean seed.

The root pushes down
        into the soil,
            down
        and down.

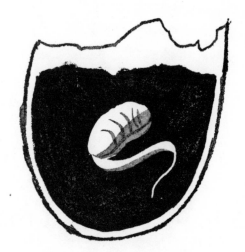

Dig up seed Number 3.

Can you see the root?

Does it look like this?

If you do not see a root, wait for another day.

Then dig up seed Number 4.

Now something else happens.

After a few more days, dig up seed Number 5.

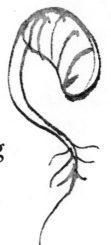

Little roots will be growing
from the big root.

They look like tiny white hairs.
They are called hair roots.

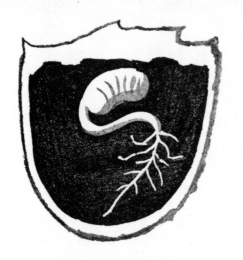

Day after day the roots
and hair roots
push down into the soil.

Day after day the bean seeds
push up and up.
They push the dirt aside.

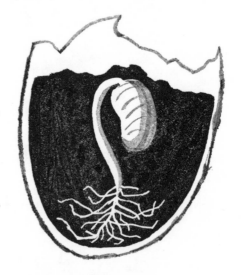

Watch your seeds.
Soon you will see shoots
push through the ground.

A shoot
is the beginning
of a green plant.

A shoot grows
toward the sun.

As a shoot pushes the bean seeds up
through the ground, the sun warms them.

As the sun warms them, the seeds break open.

Watch your seeds.

Some may have come through the ground.

Some may have broken open.

Some may look like this.

Maybe some of your seeds
have not started to grow.

How many are growing?

Count them.

The bean seeds grow fast.

 The shoots turn green.

The leaves come next.

Now your bean seeds are bean plants.

They look like this.

How many of your bean seeds are bean plants?

This is what happens to seeds.

A seed needs many things to grow.

It needs food

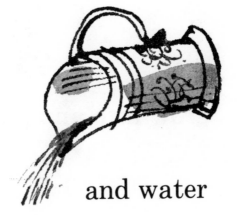

and water

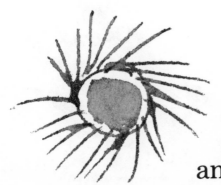

and sun.

If it has all these things, a seed will grow into a plant.

It will grow into an apple tree,   or a daisy,

or carrots,   or corn.

It will grow into clover

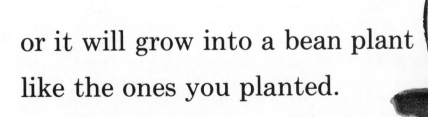

or it will grow into a bean plant
like the ones you planted.

HELENE J. JORDAN was born and educated in Grand Rapids, Michigan. She was associated with The American Museum of Natural History for eight years, for the last five of which she was executive editor of *Natural History* magazine. In 1966 she joined the Rockefeller University Press as editor, a position she held until 1971, when she began concentrating on the free-lance editing of science books for the university and for other organizations and institutions. During this period her writing-editing activities have included several other books for young people. She is married to Harry Lee Waddell and lives in New York City.

JOSEPH LOW was born in a small river town near Pittsburgh, grew up in Illinois, studied at that state's university and at the Art Students League in New York. He taught for a few years at Indiana University, then left to free-lance in New York, living in the countryside rather than in the city itself. For a time, with his Eden Hill Press, he became a printer and publisher as well as an artist. His work has been exhibited and collected by museums across the United States, in Europe, South America, and the Orient. Mr. Low and his wife now divide their year between two islands: Martha's Vineyard for summers in the north; St. John for winters in the Caribbean. In both he is able to indulge a passion for sailing.

8030706

SPI

Spirn, Michele.

In search of the
ruby sword.

IN
SEARCH
OF THE
RUBY SWORD

Written by Michele Spirn
Illustrated by Gene Feller

JANUARY
PRODUCTIONS

Library of Congress Catalog Card Number: 83-82541
ISBN: 0-934898-62-6 (library edition)
ISBN: 0-934898-74-X (paperback)

IN SEARCH OF THE RUBY SWORD

"Those were the days," said Diana Morris as she put down her book.

"What days?" asked her brother Tom, who had been watching TV in the living room while Diana read.

"The days when knights were bold and dragons ran around the countryside and magic was everywhere," said his sister.

Her twin turned off the TV set and said, "I don't know what you're talking about."

"The days of King Arthur's Court," said Diana.

"Oh, you mean King Arthur who lived long ago in England? The one that formed the Knights of the Round Table?" asked Tom.

"Right!" said Diana. "His ideas were so wonderful. There were no laws then. But King Arthur got a group of knights together to help the poor and weak. They went on quests for adventures to help those who couldn't help themselves."

"Sounds good to me," said Tom, lying back on the sofa with his feet up. "What kind of adventures did they have?"

"Exciting ones," said his twin. "There were even evil magicians, called wizards, who turned people into trees or locked them up in towers."

"Turned people into trees?" asked Tom, yawning. "Say, did this really happen?"

"Well," said Diana, hanging her head, "some of it probably wasn't true. And they're not even sure that King Arthur really lived. But I believe he did!"

"I know one way to find out," said Tom, suddenly sitting up. "Let's use the ring."

"Of course! The ring!" cried Diana. "I'll get it."

On a dig in their neighborhood, Diana had found an old black and gold ring. It was a ring that helped them travel back to the past. No one looking at it would have known that the ring hid a powerful secret. But inside, written on the band of the ring itself, was a poem: "Turn me left to go back to the past. Turn me right to get home fast."

Tom waited for Diana to get the ring. "What's taking you so long?" he yelled.

"I'm just getting some things together," she said. Finally, Diana appeared with a bag and the ring.

The twins stood close together with their hands on the ring. Tom had set it for the earliest days of British history. As he had said to Diana, "There's no real date given for King Arthur so I'll set it to the Sixth Century A.D. and hope I guess right."

Now they were ready for the trip. As they turned the ring, the lights of their home began to dim and they knew they were off on their trip back in time. It had happened this way before. Darkness fell and seemed to last for a long time. But finally, Tom and Diana started to see light.

They had landed in the middle of a great forest. Before long, a black horse galloped by. Then they heard a voice crying, "Help! Help!"

Tom and Diana ran towards the sound. Finally, they came to a clearing in the forest and saw a man, dressed in armor, lying on the ground.

"What happened?" cried Tom and Diana, as they ran over to the man.

"I fell off my horse," said the man, angrily. "I was riding along, peaceful and happy, when all of a sudden my horse jumped and started going wild. There must be some powerful magic around here. He's never acted that way before. And now I've hurt my arm and I can't continue my quest."

9

"What quest?" asked Diana.

"The quest to find the ruby sword," said the man, looking at them with surprise. "I thought everybody knew about that."

"We're strangers here," said Tom. "In fact, you might say we've just arrived."

"Oh, that explains it," said the man. "By the way, I'm Sir Garwen, a Knight of the Round Table from King Arthur's Court. Anyway, all of us are searching for the ruby sword before the evil wizard Cronin gets it. If Cronin gets his hands on the sword, the Knights of the Round Table will be finished."

"Why is that?" asked Tom.

"It's a powerful sword. Whoever uses it wins against any enemy, no matter how good a fighter that enemy is."

"That must be some sword!" exclaimed Diana.

"It is," said Sir Garwen, trying to move. "Oooh!"

"What's the matter?" asked Diana.

"I've really hurt my arm," Sir Garwen said. "I'll have to go back to Camelot and get Merlin to fix it."

"Who's Merlin?" asked Tom.

"You really must be a stranger here," said Sir Garwen. "Merlin is a powerful wizard who helps King Arthur."

"If he's so powerful, why can't he help find the ruby sword?" asked Tom.

"Oh, Merlin's funny that way. Sometimes he helps and sometimes he doesn't. This time he said it's out of his hands. He can't do anything. He keeps walking around the castle saying 'What will be, will be.' Ouch!"

"Here," said Diana. "Let me help you with your arm. I've got a scarf here that'll do the trick."

Diana pulled a scarf from her bag and made a sling for the knight's arm. When she had finished, Sir Garwen said, "Many thanks. I'll be heading back to Camelot now. By the way, where are you staying for the night?"

"We don't know," said Tom. "I'm not sure we'll be here that long."

"Well, if you need a place to stay, come to the castle," said Sir Garwen. "Everyone's welcome there. And watch out for Cronin. He loves to turn people into frogs and toads."

"Thanks," said Diana. "We'll keep that in mind."

As the knight walked away, Tom and Diana shook hands. "We made it!" they said.

"And from the looks of things, I have a feeling the ruby sword is near here," added Diana.

"What makes you think that?" asked Tom.

"Sir Garwen said he thought there was some powerful magic around here," said Diana.

"What could be more powerful than Cronin? And if Cronin is looking for the ruby sword, it must be around here."

"Uh-oh," said Tom. "I don't like that look in your eyes, Diana."

Diana smiled. "Let's have some fun and look for the ruby sword, Tom."

"Let's not and say we did," Tom answered. "Remember, Cronin's looking for it, too. And I have no wish to be turned into a frog."

"Oh, that won't happen," said Diana. "Come on, Tom."

"Well, okay," said Tom. "But the strangest things happen when we use that ring. And if I am turned into a frog, you're going to have to explain it to Mom and Dad. I can just hear you now. 'Sorry, Mom and Dad, here's Tom, your son—you may not know him because he's now a frog...but he'll be easy to feed. Just catch some flies for him. How did it happen? Well, you see there's this ring and...'"

As Tom talked, the twins walked on even deeper into the forest. Soon they came to a little stream near a large pile of rocks and stones.

"Let's sit down and have something to eat," said Diana.

"Food! You mean you brought food this time?" asked Tom.

"Sure," said Diana. "I put food in my bag. How about an apple?"

As the twins ate their apples, they looked around. It was still early in the day, but the tall trees cut off some of the light and made it darker.

"It's kind of gloomy around here," said Tom, looking around. "I wonder why that big pile of rocks and stones is there. There's nothing else like it around here."

"Let's take a look," said Diana. The twins walked over to the huge pile and looked at it closely.

"There is a small opening here," said Diana.

"Let's pull some of the rocks away and see what's inside."

It was hard work, but the twins carried away many of the rocks and stones and made an opening in the pile.

"I think we've uncovered the opening to a cave," said Diana. "Let's go in."

"How will we see in that darkness?" asked Tom.

"Simple," said Diana. "I brought a flashlight this time."

"Great!" said Tom. "Let's go."

When the twins entered the cave, they found it was much bigger than they had thought. They could easily stand up in it.

As they walked through, Tom said, "It smells like there was a fire in here. It's very smoky."

Just as he said that, the twins heard a strange sound. They jumped back. In the distance a dark shape could be seen. The twins turned and ran back to the entrance.

"Hurry!" yelled Tom. "I think something's after us. Maybe it's a dragon."

But Diana was running more slowly because she was reaching into her bag.

"What are you doing?" cried Tom, as they ran out of the cave.

"I'm getting something out to stop that creature," screamed Diana. With that, she took out a mirror and held it up in front of the dark shape.

When the creature took one look at the mirror, it screeched. It turned around and ran swiftly back through the cave.

"That was smart work!" said Tom, huffing and puffing from the run.

"Do you think it was a dragon?" Diana asked.

"Well, I don't believe in dragons but I've never seen such an animal before. That's for sure!" he replied. "And I guess it had never seen such an animal either," noted Tom.

"That's what I was counting on," sighed Diana. "I hoped it might be scared at the sight of itself for the first time."

The twins rested for a while and then decided to go back into the cave and finish exploring.

"Who knows? There might be something interesting in there," said Diana.

"As long as it's nothing interesting like strange creatures," said Tom. "Say, what do you suppose that thing was?"

The twins could come up with no good answer, but a strange thing happened as they walked farther into the cave. It became lighter and lighter instead of darker. They didn't need their flashlight any more so Diana put it back in her bag.

Soon they saw where the light was coming
from. In the corner was a long golden box that
was giving off the light.

"Wow!" I wonder what's in that box," said Diana.

"Let's open it and see," said Tom, "instead of standing here wondering about."

The box was very heavy, but finally the twins were able to open the lid. Inside, lay a golden sword that had a big red stone set in the handle.

"The ruby sword!" said Diana. "This must be it."

"We'll take it to King Arthur," said Tom, reaching in to lift it out.

"Not so fast," said a voice from behind them. "I'll take that sword now."

Turning around, the twins saw a tall, ugly man with long hair and a high, pointed hat standing there.

"Uh-oh," said Tom to himself. "I think it's toad time."

"Who are you?" asked Diana.

"Who am I? Who am I?" laughed the man. "Why I am Cronin, the most powerful, the greatest, the most evil wizard of them all...ha, ha, ha! And who might you poor, weak things be?"

While Tom stared at the wizard, Diana answered, "We're Tom and Diana, wizards from a far-off land. Certainly, you may take the sword—as long as you don't take my bag. It has all my magic in it."

"Let me look at that bag!" commanded the wizard. "Never mind the sword for now."

Diana tossed the bag to the wizard. He sat down in the cave and opened it.

"Two old apple cores," said the wizard with a snort. "You call that magic?"

"Never mind," said Diana. "Just don't look further."

The wizard came upon the mirror. He looked at himself in it. "Hmmm! A picture of a handsome fellow!" He put the mirror aside.

As Cronin looked through the bag and talked to Diana, Tom moved closer to the sword. Meanwhile, the wizard had found the flashlight. As he played with it, he pushed the button and the light came on.

"Light whenever you want it!" he said. "Now that's real magic!" He pointed the flashlight at Diana and the light picked up the glow of the ring on her finger.

"What's that?" Cronin asked. "More magic?" He reached for the ring on Diana's finger, but Tom spoke up.

"Hold it right there!" Tom had reached the sword at last. Now he picked it up and held it so the wizard could see it.

"You know that whoever holds this sword is unbeatable."

"Oh, I know," said the wizard. "But I was hoping you didn't. You've won this time, but I'll get you yet."

Cronin turned and walked out of the cave.

"Let's get out of here and give that sword to King Arthur," said Diana.

The twins walked fast and far. Soon they came to a large brown castle with towers. Flags were flying from the high walls. Tom and Diana walked up to the large gate. A man standing at the gate said, "What do you want?" Then he saw the ruby sword and let them in without another word.

Tom and Diana walked through a long hall and finally reached a big room. The room was packed with people. When they saw what the twins were carrying, they started to whisper, "The ruby sword...the ruby sword..."

In the middle of the room stood a man dressed in plain brown clothes with an old crown on his head.

"Here is the ruby sword, King Arthur," said Diana, giving it to him.

The crowd in the hall cheered. "Thank you," said the king. "We all thank you. Please make yourselves comfortable while I put the sword away for safe keeping. You will be our honored guests at the great feast we will now have."

King Arthur turned and walked out of the room. All the people came rushing up to Tom and Diana. But just then a black cat that the twins had seen in the room came and sat in front of them. As if by magic, the cat disappeared and Cronin appeared. The crowd backed away.

"I've got you now," the evil wizard said. "You no longer have the ruby sword. You're mine. But first I think I'll have a little fun. How would you like to be a frog?" he asked Tom.

As Tom moved away, he whispered to Diana. "Turn the ring!" The twins held hands and Diana turned the ring. As Cronin started the magic spell that was meant to turn Tom into a frog, the room started to fade before the twins' eyes. Soon the darkness fell and the twins went rushing forward into time.

As they stood in their own home again, Tom felt himself all over to make sure he hadn't been turned into a frog.

"Nope!" he said. "Cronin's spell didn't have time to work. We sure got out of there at the right moment."

"I'm sorry we missed the great feast," said Diana. "That would have been fun!"

As Tom stared at her, their mother called them. "Tom! Diana! Dinner! I've got your favorite—fried chicken."

Diana turned to Tom. "Just kidding," she said. "Anyway, King Arthur would have to go far to beat Mom's fried chicken!"